SEE
FELIXSTOWE
WITH ME

text and drawings by
Elizabeth-Jane Grose

First published in 2010
By Spot the Dog Press Ltd.

ISBN 978-0-9565275-0-9

Distributed by Customer Services, Suffolk Costal District Council,
Melton Hill, Woodbridge, Suffolk, IP12 1AU

Typeset and layout by Scottkirby Design Associates Ltd.
and Elizabeth-Jane Grose.

Printed and bound in Great Britain by T J International Ltd,
Trecerus Industrial Estate, Padstow, Cornwall, PL28 8RW

Acknowledgements

I am very grateful to the large number of people in Felixstowe who have contributed to this book: all those who stopped and talked to me; the dog walkers who let me photograph their canine companions; the ship spotters, who shared their knowledge; the bird watchers, particularly Nigel from the Landguard Bird Observatory, who spent a morning showing me round; Sarah Wynne and Esther Mander from Landguard Nature Reserve; Nick Marsh from Suffolk Coast and Heaths; fishermen who talked to me about their catches; Paul Rearden and the 2008 'A' Level group at Deben High School who took part in workshops I ran while I was in the early research stages of the Martello Coast Path Projects; Susan Tod at Felixstowe Museum, for fruitful discussions and cups of tea; David Morgan at Landguard Fort, with whom I have had many discussions; and all those people who turned up to the consultation days at the Town Hall and Spa Pavilion and shared their stories and memories of Felixstowe – in particular David Tolliday and Colin Tod, who checked many details for me.

Two very useful publications by Felixstowe Society were founts of information, the *Cotman Walk* and *Walking Around Felixstowe*. A special thank you must go to the Martello Coast Path Project Board, for their enthusiasm, support and encouragement – Mary Neale, Joan Sennington, Joseph James – who came up with the title for the book – Heidi Grant, Carol Mayston and Susan Robinson and her team at the Town Hall, you've all been brilliant and a pleasure to work with. Carol Gant, former Arts and Heritage Officer at Suffolk Coastal District Council, for her hard work, friendship and the loan of her bike. Thank you, Celia Page and Peter Morley-Brown, who supplied information about the signs at Felixstowe Ferry and Old Felixstowe, amongst other things.

To Rita and Jim Grose, meticulous proof readers, thank you for your grammarian expertise – any mistakes are despite your corrections!

Lastly, to Stephen, who makes everything possible.

Foreword

This enchanting book is the result of a partnership of people who have a stake in the community of Felixstowe and its Trimley neighbours working together to try to protect, improve and regenerate the quality of our environment. The Felixstowe Futures partnership has brought together Suffolk County Council, Suffolk Coastal District Council, Felixstowe Town Council, the Port of Felixstowe, the Felixstowe Chamber of Trade and Commerce, the Haven Gateway, Trimley St Martin and Trimley St Mary Parish Councils. Together the Partnership has embarked on a series of public realm projects probably only equalled in Felixstowe's history by the Urban District Council in the early years of the Twentieth Century. One of these projects is the Martello Coast Path and the Partnership was very fortunate to be able to commission the artist Lizzy-Jane Grose to provide the artwork which will be an important feature of the path. The Coast Path is emblematic of Felixstowe Futures in linking the best of the past, present and future of the town and this book, with its delightful illustrations, celebrates and records Lizzy-Jane's journey, both actual and metaphorical, along the route of the path. I hope that you will enjoy it as much as I have done.

Susan Robinson
March 2010

Preface

This is not a guide book, nor a history book, but a kind of a diary, an entirely subjective view of what I saw, what I heard, what caught my eye and the paths those things led me down during a week in December 2009 spent in Felixstowe. Think of it as a work of art, rather than the appliance of science, and I hope you will enjoy the rhythms of the words and the idiosyncrasy of the drawings, and that they will give you something of the flavour of this subtle and varied town.

Where information is given, it is true to the best of my belief, according to what people met along the way have said to me, or what I've read about Felixstowe in one of the many excellent guides and histories to be found in the local reference section of Felixstowe Library, or available at the Tourist Information Office. If, through the process of chinese whispers and interpretation, I've got things wrong, then I offer my sincere apologies.

I've always been interested in the way that myths and stories arise, often with a grain of truth that grows and changes over time. Any factual elements in this book are a bit like that – the things I've seen and heard during my week in Felixstowe are filtered through one person's perception and experience and interpreted according to my understanding. The things that I write about and draw are chosen according to what has seemed remarkable and interesting and engrossing to me – you might have chosen different things. So for example, I was struck by the number and great variety of dogs that I saw promenading with their owners as I walked around Felixstowe that December (I live in a sheep farming area, and nine out of ten dogs are collies), and thus there is a series of fifty canines of all imaginable shapes and sizes running through this book.

Felixstowe in its present form is a town that has grown and developed over a relatively short period of time (though of course its roots go way back), yet the variety of strong interests that it provokes in different people is quite striking. Seaside resort, rich with Edwardian history and stuffed with examples of late Victorian and Edwardian architecture; sandwiched between not one but two Areas of Outstanding Natural Beauty (I suppose otherwise it would be an open sandwich) as well as containing Sites of Scientific

Interest (SSIs) designated due to the rare habitat and consequent importance to wildlife; the biggest and busiest shipping port in Britain, which played a pivotal role in the political and union history of modern Britain; site of the last invasion of foreign troops on English soil with a centuries' long position of military significance; and boasting gardens that were immortalised in a poem by John Betjeman. These are all aspects of Felixstowe that people are proud of and in many cases passionately interested in. They are some of the things that caught my eye, and alongside that are the subjects that I'm interested in myself – if you like, the things I was primed to notice – like animals and birds and food and gardens and art and walking, so those form the underlying currents pulling the book along. I hope you like them too, but if not, maybe this will provoke you to do your own book about what you think is important in Felixstowe.

Elizabeth-Jane Grose
February 2010

Sunday

I arrived that December afternoon by train, as so many visitors would have done in Felixstowe's heyday. Indeed, the coming of the railway must have been one of the factors that led to Felixstowe's surge in popularity as a fashionable resort and its consequent rapid expansion. Then, as now, transport links were the key to accessibility – part of the relaxed holiday is the journey towards the destination. Trains, of course, have changed somewhat since those days – they would have been steam trains with very different carriages – the amount of space, comfort and privacy varying considerably according to the price of your ticket.

To get to Felixstowe by train now, the distant traveller must change trains at Ipswich. Here I was delayed – not because the trains weren't running on time, but because a somewhat ambiguous platform announcement had left me waiting stranded on the main concourse of platform 2, while the train pulled out of its furthest tip. Consequently I sat there muttering into yet another cup of tea in the café for another hour, full of frustrated anticipation because after so much planning and build up I wanted to ARRIVE and, most of all, to walk by the sea. I had originally wanted to make this trip in the summer, to see Felixstowe in its full holiday resort glory. It's supposed to be one of the sunniest places in Britain, and certainly this summer had enjoyed a far drier and more sunbathed July and August than we had had in the West. However, logistics and a whole host of reasons had made a summer trip impossible, and a week in December was the only option. I've always liked the sea in winter, and seaside resorts too at this time, when there is a different kind of visitor, and you get to see the town's bones with the frills of summer stripped away. Winter can be the best time, when people in the town are going about their ordinary business unimpeded by hoards of summer visitors. The wildlife changes too, bringing in many species of bird which overwinter here to escape harsher climes elsewhere in Europe.

At last the hour passed. This time I knew exactly where I had to go and stand, and boarded the short one carriage train with my fellow passengers. There was a good number of people getting on the train at Ipswich, some with suitcases. Were they, like me, heading for a winter holiday in Felixstowe, or returning home from a trip elsewhere? Certainly there was nobody with that slightly shocking bronze glow from winter sun that some wear in December. There was a cheerful look to the travellers, a brightness exemplified by the combination of a pink coat and big red suitcase as well as the multitudinous gaudily coloured shopping bags of a Sunday before Christmas.

On leaving Ipswich Station the railway winds through the industrial environs of the town, passing gaswork towers and flat-pack buildings that give way to semis and detached houses showing their backs to the train's passengers. These in turn thin out before the train dives down between rows of tall bare poplars and ash-lined embankments. The light on this side of the country is clear, dry and bright – so different from the stormy skies of recent weeks that I'd left behind. The clean, white sunlight of the winter afternoon was already fading at half-past two: the sun goes down a good half hour earlier on this coast. The train runs smoothly across fields drying out from recent rains (maybe skies have been stormy here too) and past upright poplars that nod in the breeze towards distant cross-channel cousins.

The first station stop is Westerfield, with oak and hawthorn-edged platforms. A few people get out, then we're off again across stretching fields blinking at the sun which hovers low on the horizon off to our right. Derby Road next, the sun hidden behind dark silhouettes of houses, but present still in the reflected glow on warm station brick. Here there are willow, pine and holly hedges, bright with red and green. We pull out past modern architect-designed flats and older bungalows around the edge of a wooded golf course dotted with Highland pine and silver birch. The tower of a stone church squats square and serene in the sunshine, an unchanged feature in a developing landscape. Next comes an out of town shopping "centre", the car park bursting with vehicles as people chase down bargains and life-style choices amongst the usual line-up of consumer choice provision.

All this joins seamlessly to the town itself as it spreads out towards the sea, before finally the train plunges into woodland and emerges across wet empty fields. At last we seem to have left the town behind – with the sky looming large on the flat horizon. Of course, this landscape is no more naturally formed than the townscape, having endured hundreds of years of planting, uprooting, modelling and shaping, even though it feels natural.

We stay longer at the Trimleys. The station has tubs of primulas and mixed borders of lavender, osteospermum and hydrangea, still showing the odd flower even now. The sun filtering fractured through the trees warms my window then dies behind tall spiky Christmas trees, themselves pardoned for another year, as we journey on again. The dirty windows of the train further filter the landscape. It's a beautiful afternoon to be arriving at Felixstowe, the last of the sun still lighting the sky up a bright blue from its low berth on the horizon. As we move on I get my first glimpse of the Port of Felixstowe's vast cranes. Stretching across the horizon the lifting gear of the docks appears to be hanging ready to pounce, like an immobile one-legged heron on the water's edge. Waiting.

We pull into Felixstowe's crenellated platform, cut off from the old station building by a wide car park. As we go out of the station most people head off in the direction of town, and I follow. The architecture on arrival typifies what you see in the rest of the town.

There is redbrick, solidly built with original features and decoration above, but often with the recent additions of modernisation at street level. The path out takes me through a small shopping mall in what would have once been the station building and as I emerge onto the road on the other side I see my hotel across from me. This,

the Elizabeth Orwell, is to be my home for the next week. Like the station (probably built around the same time) it's redbrick, late Victorian, framed by dark green vegetation and aflame in the last of afternoon sunshine. Inside the front door is a table display, display cabinets of things you can buy in

Felixstowe and a very ornate flower arrangement. The overall effect is classy commercialism.

The whole of the ground floor seems to be decorated in what would have been the style at the time the hotel was built. It's plush and grandiose with lots of the original features and bars called things like "his Lordship's Library" to set the tone. As you go upstairs things become a little less glamorous. The carpet pile doesn't feel quite so thick, the lighting more utilitarian than cut-glass chandelier, and in places the paintwork could use a bit of refreshment. The top-floor corridor on which my room is situated is, however, lined with original, delicately tinted watercolours of seaplanes. The subtle washes of colour are at odds with the military insignia and intended purpose of their subject matter, but entirely appropriate to the planes' airborne nature. I don't know if

they were painted by a local artist, but the subject matter, I know from my reading, is entirely appropriate, as the RAF, and the Naval Airborne division, was stationed here in Felixstowe for many years, and there was an important experimental air station in what is now part of the docks. My room is large, airy and pleasant – not one of the original hotel rooms, but obviously in a wing that was added on, with consequently bigger windows and a view across rooftops.

Leaving the unpacking and settling in for later, I head out immediately to explore the town and find the sea. By now the sun is gasping its absolute last for the day and losing the competition for brightness to the Christmas lights strung along the street. Many of the shops are open for Sunday shopping. Charity shops at the top of the road give way to butcher and banks further down. I get friendly smiles and greetings in the shops that I dip into before I succumb to the lure of the sea. My first view of the ocean is framed between buildings at the top of Bent Hill. It appears eternal, calm and luminous, twinkling in the reflected colours of the prom lights. I choose a path to the side of the Spa Gardens, a winding way down past an intriguing, turreted, white house, into the start of the Spa Gardens proper. Even in the fast disappearing light I can make out vestiges of the interesting planting that made the Gardens famous in their heyday, before it gives way to neatly maintained lawns and pampas grass. I walk along the promenade, hands in pockets against the increasing cold, past the pleasing white-boarded simplicity of Seagull and Seashell Cottages as far as Cobbolds Point. Here direct access to the coast is cut off at this point of the tide by private property on the one side, and the sea on the other. By this point (point of time as well as geography), my nose has joined by fingers in complaining at the increasing chill, so I decide to turn back (mental note: must remember to buy gloves in the morning, stupid to come on a walking holiday without, and I'd left my woolly hat behind). By now there were buoys winking at me from the sea, and the lights of boats sitting stationary on the horizon as they wait to come into port. I sit for a minute on one of the sunshine design benches (Felixstowe, Sunshine Capital) and watch a fisherman setting his bait by torchlight, with his young assistant huddled under a windbreak waiting for Dad to catch something. It is too cold to linger, and I decide to strike uphill, hoping to build up a bit of warmth as I climb, and thinking I might find a more direct, if less picturesque route back.

In fact, there's lots to see along the way, particularly in terms of architecture. I go past a vast and decorated building, whose arched entrance proclaims it to be Harvest House. In front of it a petrified and bashful boy stands on what was presumably a fountain, under a lamp, holding a piece of cloth between his legs, which inadequate cover makes me shiver just to look at him. The building's patterned brickwork is undoubtedly fine, with neo-Tudor shapes and leaded windows attesting to the care and expense of the original building work. I can hear strains of music in the distance in the direction I'm headed, and guess it is probably the evening service of some church, but as I get closer I see people streaming into a building with four uniformed musicians outside, playing Christmas Carols. All are playing brass and I don't know how they manage to keep their fingers working in the cold. It sounds and looks very Christmassy and cheerful, and I walk smiling on, humming *Good King Wenceleslas* to myself as I make my way back to the hotel.

23

Monday

Today I'm going to walk the Martello Coast Path, which runs for approximately five and a quarter miles from the docks Viewing Area on the mouth of the River Orwell to Felixstowe Ferry at the mouth of the River Deben. These two rivers frame the land that Felixstowe sits upon, and have undoubtedly played an important role in the development of the settlements and moorings from which Felixstowe has grown. The walk is a great introduction to Felixstowe. As it follows the seashore it inexorably unfolds the range of different things the sea has brought to the town, and which have caused it to develop in such a variety of ways. From the southern-most end of the path you start with the Port (which now dominates the town) then an early taste of military history with Landguard Fort (which used to dominate the town), cheek-by-jowl with important wildlife habitats on Landguard Point. Then on past Martello Towers along the Prom and the sea-side resort proper, with a built and formal landscape of gardens and Victorian/Edwardian architecture, past Cobbolds Point and inland, through more examples of grand houses and hotels from the same era and out through the "wilds" of the golf course to the smaller and older settlement of Felixstowe Ferry.

First things first, however, as there is a chill wind blowing straight off the North Sea, so down to the High Street to buy a woolly hat and some gloves. Then a bus which takes me most of the way down towards the docks, leaving me to walk the last stretch along

Viewpoint Road.

The walk proper starts in the car park at the Viewing Point for the docks at Landguard Point. In summer you can also get a foot and bicycle ferry across to Harwich and Shotley from here, connecting you up to walks along the Essex coast. I'm a bit of a sucker for information boards, and there's a good one in the car park telling you about nature reserves in the area (Landguard and Trimley Marshes), the Port, military history, museums (Landguard Fort and Felixstowe Museum) and Landguard Bird Observatory. From this Viewing Point you look out over the Orwell estuary and the north bank of the River Stour onto part of the Suffolk Coast and Heaths Area of Outstanding Natural Beauty (AONB).

More than 3.5 million 20ft containers of cargo and a million passengers pass up here every year to the Haven Ports of Felixstowe, Harwich, Ipswich and Mistley. There are actually two dock terminals here at Landguard. The first, Landguard Terminal was built in 1967, a deepwater facility for container ships, then later in 1986 the first phase of Trinity Terminal was added - with a second phase in 2007 – a newer, bigger dock with twenty-four cranes and spanning 1.5 miles. This has recently been extended again and has a continuous quay front of 2,354 metres and 27 cranes. Because of the way the sea and river wash silt into the mouth of the estuary, the deep-water channel has to be continually scoured to a depth of 14.5 metres – there is a dredger at work as I stand and watch. It's this deep water channel which is so important, allowing the big ships up the estuary, which has also in the past made this a strategically important spot that needed to be guarded against enemy attack.

The Port of Felixstowe is now owned by a multi-national company, under the umbrella "Hutchison Whampoa Limited". The first port company was founded in 1875, under the name of the "Felixstowe Railway and Pier Company" by Colonel George Tomline, who obtained an Act of Parliament to construct a tidal dock in 1879 – the first sod was dug in 1881. The dock basin was 600 x 300 foot, surrounded by corn mills, granaries and maltings which were big industries locally, and consequently had goods to export. At the time cargoes were transported by sailing barges and schooners. The first commercial cargo that was unloaded on Tomline's new quay was 471 tons of coal, on 7th April 1886, from the SS Crathie out of Scotland. In 1910 the haven was also a base for torpedo boats and destroyers, with a significant Naval and Air Force presence spanning both World Wars. Huge floods in 1953 devastated the dock, which needed extensive renovation. Somewhere, lost beneath a wave of development, is the site of the Dooley Fort, Martello Tower "N". Since then it has seen ships from all over the world - Scandinavia, Iceland, Germany, the US, Holland, France, Ireland, Spain, Portugal, Malta, Italy, Tunisia, Libya, Greece,

Turkey, the Lebanon and, above all, the Far East.

As well as ships and all things military, the estuary is also of great importance to wildlife, so the Viewing Point is good for bird spotting as well as ship spotting. In fact, it's of such importance that there are international designations set up to protect this habitat. Up to 50,000 waders and wildfowl over-winter on the Stour and Orwell, searching in the estuary mud for snails, worms and shrimps. Even in the car park itself I saw little gulls, turnstones, ringed plover and starlings.

As I stand looking out across the estuary I can just make out Walton-on-the-Naze in the distance. There are tugs and pilot boats beetling about, as well as the dredger. There are also dozens of people standing around like me, or, given the cold, sitting in their cars watching ships coming in and out. I'd heard of train spotting, but ship spotting was a new one on me! I wondered how it worked, and got talking to a couple of my neighbours. The first thing I learn is that the container ships are called "box boats" by those in the know – it's always satisfying to get the terminology right. "Box boats" are a surprisingly recent invention – the first container ships were made from converted tankers, of which there was a surplus after World War II. Then in the 1950s they started to make purpose built container ships, which now carry approximately 90% of all non-bulk cargo (that's most of the world's exported manufacturing goods) all around the globe. According to Wikipedia, there are plans to build a container ship capable of carrying 22,000 20ft (or equivalent) containers, which at 450 metres long and 60 metres wide would make it the biggest ocean-going vessel in the world. These huge boats need only a handful of men for crew – it must feel like being the only inhabitant in a deserted village. The one I saw being guided in by the diminutive Harwich Harbour Pilot seemed incredibly huge, dwarfing the coastline and carrying unimaginable quantities of stuff. Seeing the size of the boats, and the vast cranes needed to unload them, one has to wonder what we do with all this stuff, and whether we really need to be sending it around the world with diesel engines. 35% of all UK container cargo passes through Felixstowe.

On a more sustainable note, I could see some huge towers for wind turbines sitting on the nearest bit of quay, and my instructor, who was telling me about the ships, said that these were waiting to be taken over to the Harwich side for assembly, then on to an offshore wind farm. I asked him, with the huge numbers of ships that go in and out of the Port, whether there were many accidents.

Apparently there have been very few – one collision and sinking offshore, one when a ship ran onto the shingle out on Landguard Point, and one where a captain apparently (or allegedly) decided that he knew better than the Harbour Pilot, that the channel was deep enough to take his ship all the way up to Ipswich, and then found that he'd run out of water.

There is a memorial at the Viewing Point - not for lost sailors, but lost airmen - the crew of a Hampden Medium bomber (known as "flying coffins") who died on June 4th 1940 as they returned from a bombing raid over Holland, when their plane hit a barrage balloon cable and crashed into the sea. In 1995 workers on an extension to Trinity Terminal discovered mangled wreckage of the plane and a human jawbone as they dredged the seabed.

Leaving the Viewing Point car park I pass Felixstowe Museum, generally open only between Easter and the October half term, but also out of hours by appointment, so I decide to try to make an appointment for later in the week. It's a museum of local, social and military history. Next-door is the imposing Landguard Fort, the last fort in England to have repelled a full-scale invasion attempt, and the latest incarnation of a line of fortifications which date back to the mid-Sixteenth Century, to guard the mouths of the rivers and the deep-water channel.

I turn then into the open space of Languard Point, and the Nature Reserve, past a notice about the Bird Observatory. The land looks quite scrubby, very open to the elements and the blustery wind – I read somewhere that this area at the mouth of the Orwell was once held to be a bee paradise, due to the extensive heathland habitat. Rabbits hop disconsolately between overgrown tufts of bramble bushes, but the views are amazing – I walk up to the top of what looks like a dune, but is in fact the remnants of a butt, built to stop shot during shooting practice, and look out over an expanse that stretches across the docks, the Fort, a row of fishermen along the shingle and extends along the coast itself from Walton-on-the-Naze up and across Felixstowe to Cobbolds Point. The North Sea is carrying on its relentless pounding of the shingle coast, urged on by a cold wind, above the even colder looking depths. I shiver, thinking of those three airmen from the Viewing Point Memorial in their icy graves and am glad that I'm not one of those out there "in peril on the sea".

Leaving Landguard Common I emerge onto Manor Terrace. One family died here when a WWII training flight crashed into their cottage. It was also part of the area that was badly affected by the 1953 floods which swept across from the Orwell estuary. Seeing the absolute flatness of land between here and the sea, it doesn't take much imagination to picture what might happen if sea levels really are set to rise. Along Manor Terrace on the right-hand side I come across Landguard Lodge, where Tomline (he who built the first docks) had his "Manor House". There's a very interesting notice board attached to the wall, with cuttings about local history (I learnt that Landguard Fort used to be regarded as being part of Essex, not Suffolk and that there is currently risk of invasion by Sargassum muticum – also known as japweed, wire weed or strangle weed), tide tables and a Harbour Map for the Haven.

At the end of Manor Terrace I turn again towards the sea and join the southern end of the Promenade, lined with brightly painted beach huts of yellow, indigo and cobalt blue, firmly shut against the winter weather. There's been extensive work here recently to shore up the land against coastal erosion – indeed the length of the prom is lined by a sea wall. Here huge piles of boulders are heaped up in rows, some bearing drill lines marking where they were riven from their stone bed. They are alien, dark grey rocks, their bases smothered by encroaching sand in contrast to the shingle which predominates down at Landguard Point. The problem of coastal erosion is not a new one – in 1902 Felixstowe and Walton UDC erected a granite wall at a cost of £36,000 "to halt erosion" - and a 19th Century writer comments: *"Along this line of coast from Deben to the Stour it (the North Sea) has been advancing with some rapidity, and in the course of the nineteenth century considerable alterations in the disposition of the land and water may have taken place, and so much is this the case, that it is permissible to conjecture that in the Roman period a tract of saltmarshes stretched across the present opening of the Harwich Haven."*

One survivor of all this coastal erosion is Martello Tower "P", now part of the National Coastwatch Institution, housing the Felixstowe Coastal Surveillance Station, where volunteers look out for shipping, or anything, in distress on the water. In front of Martello

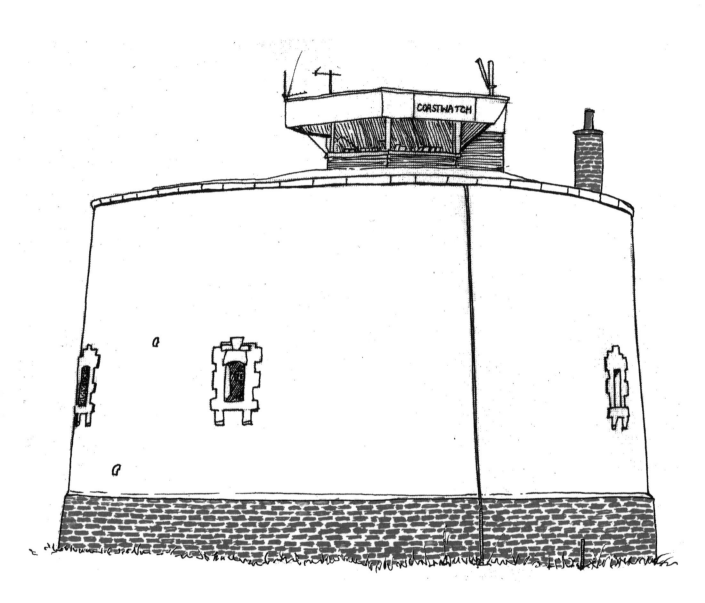

Tower "P" a County Wildlife site is roped off – home to stinking goosefoot (a rare shingle plant) which apparently is found at only three sites in the UK; this is one and Landguard Point another. Vegetated shingle is a very rare habitat, and this bit of the coast still has some. It is of international importance, providing a home for the yellow horned poppy, sea kale and the sea pea and the small copper butterfly, amongst others. Vegetated shingle plants have deep tap roots to reach fresh water, and leathery waxy leaves, to stop them losing it. Presumably these deep roots help in turn to stabilise the shingle against erosion.

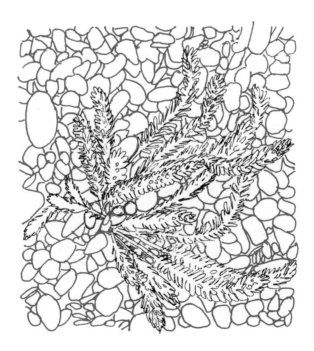

Then onwards past more brightly coloured but determinedly shut beach huts, until I reach the pier, which had been dominating the skyline as I walked along the prom. The pier is now rather a sorry affair; only the mouth of it is open, with various noisy arcade games. Once upon a time it received thousands of visitors who landed from the Belle paddle steamers onto the pier when they came for a day out in Felixstowe. In Edwardian times the bathing resort stretched for a mile in each direction from the pier, where there was nearby a dance pavilion and bandstand too. During World War II the pier was bombed in the middle to stop enemy landings, as well as having anti-tank traps and trenches dug into the beach underneath.

By now I feel like I've walked a good distance, and am also freezing cold, so I leave the promenade, where all the food booths are closed, and head across the road to one of the many cafés. I choose Joe Crowley's, which has a colourful window and amazing display of ice creams. The proprietor chats to me as I eat – I'm the only customer on this cold Monday lunchtime – telling me about the café, which is in the style of an American diner complete with soda stream, and regales me with stories of famous customers. By the time I leave the café and walk back to the prom it's high tide, and a rough sea besides, with waves reaching almost up to the prom itself.   The route here takes me past the War Memorial (with a bird, presumably the dove of peace, perched on top) and the Town Hall. I make a mental note to pop into the Tourist Information Office the next morning, and get their take on what I should do during my week in Felixstowe. There are quite a few walkers about, some along the promenade, or some further back in the Spa Gardens, mostly older couples or parents with small children, and dog-walkers of great variety and profusion (the dogs, not the owners).

I sit for a moment in one of the beautiful Edwardian shelters which line the promenade - this one cream-painted wood and glass - each one different, and watch sets of big brown and white waves pounding the shingle, leaving clumps of seaweed and bits of rubbish behind. I feel even colder just looking at the spray, and move on to warm up. A little further along, the waves actually start to come over the promenade itself, and I pass one mum and dad both pushing pushchairs; parents and older toddler alike equally delighted at their near drenching. The sea does endlessly delight, surprise and scare us. Even on a day like today, when it is threatening and inhospitable, it is still ceaselessly and unpredictably changing, and unwittingly interacting with us as we try our luck with it. I reach the end of the prom, and there's clearly no way of walking along the shore past Cobbolds Point - the waves are up and across the road at this juncture. I'd been told by locals

that the beach just here is a great place for beachcombing, presumably something to do with the action of longshore drift dumping objects on a ridge of land before moving on, but no chance of that today. Whatever the mechanics of it, I'd been told that such treasures as sharks' teeth, bits of World War II planes and amber have turned up here. It was also around this spot that the Dutch landed their invasion force on the 2nd July 1667, under the command of one Admiral de Ruyter. They then marched back along the route I had just walked, some two and a half miles, presumably to try and capture Landguard Fort. One account I read said that de Ruyter landed 5,000 men, another 1,600, and that they were repelled by a force of 500 men under Captain Nathaniel Darrell, and that July 2nd is called Darrell day in his honour.

It was a relief to turn my back on the sea and the wind, and walk up Maybush Lane. Locally, however, there is a very strong desire that the Martello Coast Path should stick to the coast, and a way be found to extend the path around Cobbolds Point, though the land above is owned by a large private house, with razor wire fences. Perhaps the next round of coastal erosion works will provide the opportunity to engineer continuous public access to the shoreline. Anyway, for now, up Maybush Lane, where the houses are altogether bigger and grander than their cousins towards the southern end, with ornate decoration and garages with electrically operated doors.

I walk along Golf Road, with a strip of green and trees between me and the sea. I think this is the site of Brackenbury Fort, an anti-aircraft battery built around 1910 and demolished in the 1960s. In World War I Felixstowe was twice attacked by enemy aircraft, and thirty people were killed. I plunge back down concrete ramps that zig-zag the cliff, emerging between rows of candy painted beach huts to the sea again. The waves are now so threatening that I walk hugging the curved sea wall, flinching into it every time a wave hits.

A woman walks past me in the opposite direction, grinning from ear to ear, "Isn't it amazing?" she asks.

I scuttle up levels between beach huts (how many of them get press-ganged by the sea each winter?) until I come to a stretch where a bank of shingle intercedes between the sea and me. The relief! Now I can enjoy the drama at a safe distance. Thinking back to the 19th Century commentator's cogitations on the way the sea changes the coast, I can see anew that now, today, there is still a sense of shifting patterns of landscape, that the margins are not fixed or mappable. That land does travel. I come to what is known locally as the "Dip", a favourite spot with local wind and kite surfers, though not today! Here drawn into the sea wall is part of an artwork by Simon Read. Called "To Forgotten Fleets", silhouettes of ships made by etching concrete with blasted sand – now being smoothed away again as the North Sea hurls pebbles and sand at the ships, and by the action of the water itself against them – like real ships battered by the sea. The ships appear and disappear with your angle of sight. The smallest is less than 10 centimetres high, and the largest well over a metre. I've talked to people who've lived in Felixstowe for years, and walked the path a hundred times, and never noticed this subtle and elegant artwork.

I'm on the home stretch of my day's walk by now, and the light is starting to fade already. I come in sight of my second Martello

Tower of the day, nested between golf course and sea, with an abandoned, blank-faced, neglected air. In the distance I can see a third tower, this one with a light on top, and windows set in, looking altogether more cheerful. To my right now the shingle is heaped into dunes, the highest even with a faint blush of green on top. The golf course itself is completely deserted, not a single addict at play. The last stretch of the path alongside the golf course interposes more massive sea defence boulders between the sea and me – they're crowned with sand – presumably evidence that the sea does sometimes come up over the top and deposit it there, and a few stubborn plants cling tenaciously in crevices between boulders.

On coming abreast with the third Martello Tower I see that it is in fact somebody's home, with three lit windows, two chimneys and aerials; somehow even the outer walls themselves look more decorative than the brooding example I'd passed half a mile back. This is the start of Felixstowe Ferry, the end of my walk, and I'm welcomed in by the rapturous applause and melodious fluting of the wind through dozens of metal masts and the ringing, bell-like, of lanyards slapping against masts – the parking lot for the sailing club. I can see picturesque beach bungalows snuggled up next to the sailing club, a couple of pubs and a café. But I've no time to explore. I've timed it perfectly and there's a bus waiting by the Ferryboat Inn to ferry me back to town. I'll come back and explore later in the week.

TUESDAY

Tuesday

I decide to start the day at the Tourist Information Office, to get the full low down on what there is to do in Felixstowe. The office is next to the Town Hall, a decorative red brick building on the sea front, which I'd walked past yesterday. It was built in 1892 and recently restored. It's a handsome building which holds one-off art exhibitions and has occasional open days for people to look around.

On my way down to the Tourist Information Office, I stop at the top of the hill above the Town Hall at a spot called the Wolsey Gardens Lookout. There are fine views from here (in fact there's a sign that says "Welcome to Felixstowe, the best 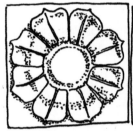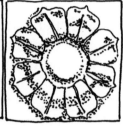 view of the sea") and a telescope you can put your money into to watch the ships go by. There's also an artwork, "The Captain's Table" by Colin Gilbert, set into the ground, surrounded on one side by railings that are inset with ships' wheels and topped with starfish and on the other by scallop shell benches. It's this kind of detail that sets the space apart, gives it character and playfulness. The floor-based element of the artwork consists of a bronze plaque enclosed within a " Nautilus" sea shell design created from pavers and concrete. The plaque bears a map, situating Felixstowe in relation to the geography of the North Sea, and telling us that Aberdeen is 361 miles away and Shanghai 9,200. Presumably these are all places that ships come or go to from the Port of Felixstowe. There's also an interesting extract from the "Nautical Almanac", about a local sea captain, Thomas Cavendish from Trimley, who set out in July 1586 with 123 men aboard three galleons, the Desire, the Content and the Hugh Gallant, to try their fortunes as privateers on the High Seas. Their voyage took them some 30,000 miles and two years, circumnavigating the globe looking for "profit and opportunity". From the Canary Islands to Sierra Leone, Brazil, Peru, The Philippines, South Africa and St Helena they raided coastal settlements and attacked Spanish vessels, including looting the Santa Anna, a much bigger 700 ton Spanish galleon of silk and gold. They had to scuttle the Hugh Gallant off South America, due to losses from the crew, but those who survived the trip arrived back in England in 1588, the year of the Spanish Armada.

I walk down through the Wolsey Gardens, past many Canary Island plants, as well as phormiums, lavender and santolina in box-edged beds. The lady at the Tourist Information is friendly and welcoming, asking about my hotel and whether I'm comfortable there. I say that I am interested in walking, gardens, wildlife and music, and ask what she would recommend in the area for the next week. On the music front, there is little on offer, only a big band night at the Spa Pavilion on Friday. It's not a form of music I know anything about, but I usually enjoy anything live, so I decide to give it a go. On the walks front, there are various maps of the town, a listing for "Health Walks" in the area – these are walks with local leaders, where you can do a walk, be sociable and get exercise at the same time. I decide against this one, as it is along a two mile stretch of part of the Martello Coast Path which I had done the day before. The location of Trimley Marshes Nature Reserve and how to get there isn't very clear, but I do get two very useful looking publications, both put out by the Felixstowe Society – one called *The Cotman Walk* looking at notable architecture, mostly designed by the architect Thomas W Cotman. The other booklet is entitled *Walking Around Felixstowe*, all pretty much circular walks, and I decide to start my day with one of these.

Walk number 7 is one I can start practically from where I stand outside the Tourist Information Centre. The book calls it "Town and Coast". I'd done the Landguard portion of the walk the previous day, so I decide to leave that out, as I'm also intending to go back and spend more time on Landguard Point tomorrow. I cross the

road in the direction of the Leisure Centre – outside this building Suffolk Coastal District Council put together an annually changing floral sculpture – this year's is a mermaid crossed with an octopus, designed by local school girl Jenny Meredith from Deben High. I'm told that last year's was a Spitfire, in honour of it being the 50th anniversary of the granting of the freedom of Felixstowe to RAF Felixstowe. Heading out along the Promenade, I 'm struck by how different the sea is today under a blue sky. Calm, measured waves (still more grey-brown than blue, though) politely lap the shore, with no hint of yesterday's dramas and tantrums. Past the various amusements, all shut up for the off-season, the wall lined with recently trimmed tamarisk hedges. I read in the *Cotman Walk* booklet that tamarisk was first brought to England by Philip

Thicknesse, one of the governors of Landguard Fort - there's certainly a lot of tamarisk to be seen in this area.

I stop to talk to one of the fishermen near the pier. It seems a popular occupation along here in all weathers, with some fishermen handling two rods at once. This chap said that he often caught bass, cod (at night) and sole near the pier, but mostly just enjoyed sitting out there, and thought that watching the sea was better than the telly.

One thing I missed yesterday on my way past (probably I was staring out to sea, or had my head down trying to avoid the full blast of the wind) was Manning's Amusement Arcade – itself a striking 30s style building in pink, white and blue – topped by a light, airy and above all whimsical clock of spirals and Mickey Mouse. The story I've been told about this clock is that it was originally designed as a water-clock, commissioned from the highly original Tim Hunkin – who has contributed such anarchic brilliance to the restoration of Southwold Pier – to be placed in the Spa Gardens in Felixstowe, but maintenance issues caused it to be removed, and it

fish and chips rock candyfloss ice cream popcorn FAMILY FUN CENTRE

would have disappeared altogether if Mannings hadn't offered it a home atop their façade.

On past Martello Tower 'P' which I get to see from the back today too. It has quite a forbidding aspect; I guess all the Martello Towers do, after all they were designed for defence of the realm and to withstand attack by Napoleon. There were twenty-nine towers built along the East Coast between 1803 and 1812. The five mile stretch of the Martello Coast Path is, or would have been, home to eight towers, labelled "N" to "U', two of these have been lost to the sea, the remains of another demolished during port development, fragments of a fourth incorporated into a new building, and four - 'P", 'Q", 'T" and 'U' - still clearly visible and little changed. From the Langer Road side I can see that the door (apparently the only entrance) for 'P' is some five metres above the ground. Apparently the men garrisoned there had to climb up via a rope ladder, which could then be pulled up to keep the enemy out. Twenty odd men would man each tower, living on the first floor, with perhaps a hundred kegs of gunpowder stored on the floor beneath them! There was a revolving panel on the top floor, so that the guns could be turned to follow their target.

Rather than go directly up Beach Station Road, (along with Manor Terrace one of the streets built speculatively by Colonel Tomline when he was trying to encourage the town to develop towards his new docks at the southern end), I do a short detour along Langer Road and back to have a look at the 1953 Flood Memorial – a commemorative garden with artwork by pupils from Langer School with artists Rosemary Humphries and Claire Curtis. A bronze plaque with text by Andy Smith tells the tragic story of how forty-one people died on the night of 31st January 1953, when a severe depression over the North Sea combined with gale force onshore winds and a high point of the natural tide cycle to cause a massive tidal surge, which was particularly devastating in this part of Felixstowe. The water reached a height of 1.8 metres. For me a very effective part of the artwork is a simple blue line set into the rear wall to show how high this was. Although many people managed to escape up onto the roofs of their houses they subsequently died of exposure in the bitter weather.

I retrace my steps in sombre mood to the entrance of Langer Park, which runs parallel to Langer Road. The park is a pleasant green space, with a children's playground and some striking palms, but not spectacular in itself. There's a railway running along beside the park, and near the park's entrance is the site of Colonel Tomline's Beach Station, which he must have hoped would bring so many visitors to his new resort.

Everywhere in the town are reminders of the military past – here in the name of the Ordnance Hotel which stands on Garrison Lane, recalling the gun battery which once stood where the entrance to the pier now is.

Up Orwell Road and past St John's Church (featured in Betjeman's poem *The Last of Her Order*), a redbrick Victorian erection with a tall robust spire which appears somehow disjointed from the rest of the building, as though it was added at a different time. My last stop on the walk is another Martello Tower, this one, 'Q", converted to a private dwelling, so I can only peer at it between trees and shrubs from the gateway. It looks well-maintained, and I think myself that it is better for ancient monuments to be used, because that way someone has an interest in keeping them upright. I like to think of buildings having different phases in their lives, and it's pleasing that this one, built for war, should have retired into domesticity.

I decide to spend the rest of the day around the town, doing the Cotman Walk. First though, I head up to the Library for a little more local research. Everybody should visit the Library! Not only is it the place if you want to get information on local history, it's also a contemporary art gallery and has a good café. The staff are friendly and helpful, and you're not frowned at if your mobile goes off or something. You can get your news fix from the telly in the café, or log on for internet time while you sip your cappuccino. You can also get lunch – sandwiches, jacket potatoes and home-made cakes.

The artwork on display is threefold. There are some sumptuous large-scale photographs of Felixstowe in all its variety. These were, I am told, done by "someone who worked for the Council". The colours are rich and luscious and I particularly like one which captured a geometric grid of red and green shipping containers, themselves further divided to form grids within grids, like a Mondrian gone mad. The colour hegemony of single prime and corresponding complementary colour is broken by the happy accident of a single blue container in the bottom right hand corner. It makes me think of all sorts of things, the sheer volume of STUFF that is being shipped around the world to be consumed by us, the lives of the people in far-away lands who make and sell all this stuff, Michael Wolf's scary photographs of dense, colour coded tower-block housing in Hong Kong and the sometimes constricting structures of modern lives.

The Library has etched glass windows showing marine life, and the third artwork, a very jaunty, quirky steel sculpture of grumpy seagulls perched on a vertically hung net. This is by Paul Richardson, a Suffolk-based artist, and is almost a caricature of seagulls. The humorous look of the piece belies the skill necessary to bend the steel into these expressive shapes, and it's altogether idiosyncratic and original.

The Cotman Walk starts from a familiar spot, the road between the station and my hotel. They are in fact the first two buildings of note on the walk. I learn from the book that the station was not in fact designed by Cotman, but by one Mr. Ashby, and that the original 500 foot canopy has been cut in half to provide car parking. The hotel was built in 1896, for Douglas Tollemache, who was looked down on by his aristocratic relations because he set himself up as a brewer and hotelier. Perhaps they became less disapproving when he ended up supporting the family through his business interests. There's a very nice stone pineapple on the wall outside the hotel – pineapples were once a bit of a status symbol, with grand families competing to see who could grow them.

The area around Constable and Gainsborough Roads is known locally as the 'Artists' Quarter', and on Gainsborough Road I find the Reunion Gallery, whose windows are a multi-coloured treasure box amidst the surrounding solid redbrick Victoriana. It's run by local artists and shows a mixture of art and craft objects, providing a showcase for more local artists. You can get coffee in the courtyard, purchase a local landscape or some beautiful craft (I bought a little gold bird to go on the Christmas tree).

Back on the Cotman Walk, I find that it is in individual details, rather than the overall architecture that a lot of the pleasure lies for me. These days whoever commissions buildings is generally trying to push the price down to such an extent that there's no budget left for decoration or anything whose sole function is to please the eye. I found it slightly distracting trying to look at things and read the book at the same time, and I think it's more my nature to wander around and see what catches my eye. The book does give me a route to follow, though, and it's very good on background, history and details. It tells you to look out for things you might otherwise miss, but for me after a while I get rather bogged down by the feeling that looking at what I'm told to look at is rather like having to do one's homework! One of the buildings I find striking in this section of the walk is the stable block on Bath Road. A pretty imposing place to keep the horses. These architect designed stables were built for the Bath Hotel, itself burned down by the suffragettes in April 1914. This was supposed to be "the last violent act" by the suffragette movement. The hotel was patronised

by the wealthy and politically important, and no doubt seen as a prominent target in the area. I turn the corner of Bath and Orwell Roads and see the sea. A heart-lift moment! Down the hill and on my left, the remains of the Bath Hotel are supposed to have been incorporated into the Bartlet Hospital, which is on the suggested detour, and is also supposed to incorporate a remnant of Martello Tower 'R', though it's not visible from the outside. I walk on past Seagull and Seashell Cottages, which I find much more pleasing in their simplicity and symmetry than a lot of the grander houses. The decoration on these cottages is in select details, wavy eaves-end gabling and the fringe under the balcony. Though someone has added a very fancy block work wall and iron gates. I stop for a cup of tea at Mrs. Simpson's, formerly the stables (or attached to the former stables, perhaps) of the next-door Fludyer Arms, and designed again by Cotman. It's warm enough to sit outside in the sunshine, unlike

yesterday when the wind was blowing a gale and the waves coming up over the road and spraying passers-by with white foam. Today I look out over a calm sea at Sealand out in the distance, looking like a megalithic stone structure on water. This is a former World War II fort, six miles off the Suffolk coast, whose current owners claim that it is an independent nation.

Up Maybush again, the most striking building here is Cranmer House, which apparently started life as a fisherman's cottage. Countless additions give it the higgledy-piggledy stuck together look which I always associate with Victorian architecture: Tudor-look chimneys atop Flemish gabling. The Victorians did own much of the world, so it is not surprising that they felt so free to borrow architectural styles from other places and other times. Cranmer House speaks of wealth and privilege, and in fact you can't get too close as it is a private residence. It was one of the buildings, like many on the Cotman Walk in this section, which were used by Felixstowe College, a private girls' school which closed in 1994. On the way back from the detour I give in to the urge to go off piste for a while, and wander along streets whose architecture is, to my eye, as pleasing and decorative as those on the official walk.

Returning to the route proper, Harvest House, which I'd noticed my first afternoon in Felixstowe, is a truly impressive building. There is pleasing decorative brick and ornamental stonework. Flights of fancy are added via domed turrets. It was built by Cotman for the same Douglas Tollemache who commissioned what is now the Elizabeth Orwell Hotel. It was once the Felix Hotel, the grandest hotel of Felixstowe's heyday, with fifty two bathrooms, private putting green, squash courts and a palm court amongst the amenities for guests. In the 1950s it was sold to Fisons, the fertiliser company. The local artificial fertiliser industry, of which Fisons had long been a part, had roots in the discovery of coprolite in Felixstowe, at the base of the cliffs near Cobbolds Point, around 1843. The phosphate nodules that made up the coprolite (including fossilized dinosaur dung) were taken to a building on

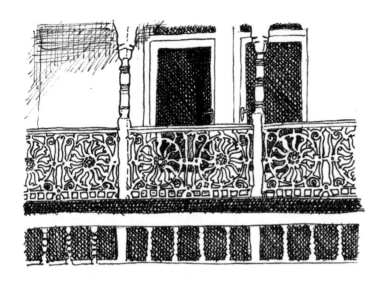

what is now called Coprolite Street, and crushed with sulphuric acid to make fertiliser. Apparently it smelt terrible.

Cotman was the nephew of the famous watercolourist, who painted so many subtle watercolours of East Anglia. Cotman the younger was certainly a prolific architect, who worked in a variety of styles. The things I remember most about the rest of the walk are details like the white wrought iron balconies on one of the houses on Hamilton Gardens (the Empress of Germany stayed in one of these houses when she visited, giving Felixstowe the royal seal of approval and adding enormously to its fashion status), the italianate white elegance of South Beach Mansion and then walking up Hamilton Road, lifting my eyes above high street level to the wealth of detail in ridge tiles, fluting, masks and lion's heads. The book captures it perfectly – *"an exuberance of detailing"*.

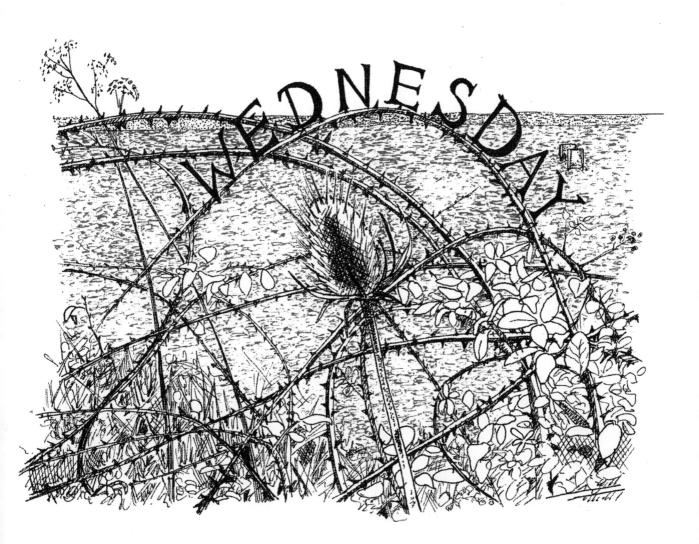

Wednesday

After the previous day circling around the town, I want to spend the next couple of days exploring aspects of either end of the Martello Coast Path. There are buses, but they're not frequent in winter, so I arrange to borrow a bike. Cycling is a great way to get around the town. Apart from a couple of notable exceptions the coast is pretty flat, and there are routes which form part of the National Cycle Network. There are bikes for hire at Felixstowe Ferry, and also from a bike shop in town, though I had no joy at the latter ("it's off season"), so I end up borrowing a bike from fellow artist and Felixstowe resident Carol Gant, who has also contributed anecdotes and encouragement to the creation of this book.

The military has played a significant role in Felixstowe's history, and the most obvious remaining manifestation of this today is Landguard Fort, down by the docks. It was built there to protect the deep-water channel, that inroad to the country, and commands views for miles in each direction. The first fort was proposed in 1539, when the site was inspected by Henry the VIII himself, and there has been a fort there since 1543. The current fort incorporates large portions

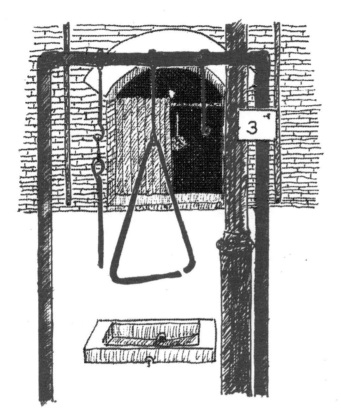

that were built in the mid 1700s with later additions, particularly in the Victorian period and the 20th Century. In the 1700s, the peninsula would flood and the main link to land was a boat to Harwich. Talk about building on the floodplain! It's difficult to imagine the great determination – or desperation - which drove such a major building project under such difficult conditions.

I'm shown the paintings room, and given a potted history of some of the subjects by David Morgan, Operations Manager at Landguard Fort. Portraits of past governors predominate: there's the Earl of Holland, first governor of the fort; Colonel West; and, perhaps the most controversial of all, Philip Thicknesse, soldier and writer of travel books, whose running battles with Tobias Smollett filled the press of the day.

Thicknesse was famous for his quarrels, and fell out with both his two sons. He wrote his life story, entitled *The Autobiography of Philip Thicknesse, Governor of Landguard Fort and unfortunate father of George, Baron T....*, and notoriously bequeathed his left hand to his son, with whom he hadn't shaken hands in many years. He met Gainsborough, supposedly at Landguard Fort in 1754, and became something of a patron of the painter: there was even a Gainsborough painting hung in the Fort itself, which has since been lost. The fort still has a strong arts programme, with installations by contemporary artists, exhibitions of photography and the occasional music event. Henry Williamson, who wrote "Tarka The Otter", was stationed at Landguard as a deputy adjutant in World War II. There are also battle re-enactments, and "paranormal investigations" – Landguard is believed to be inhabited by a number of resident ghosts.

The architecture of the fort is very particular, quite unlike any other building I have entered. Obviously it reflects the purpose for which it was built (that of defence) and this use was very singular and is still very visually striking. I wander around the ground floor, down dark, winding corridors whose levels mysteriously go up and down, going in at one point in the outer wall, and being disgorged into the central courtyard. It is only when I look at the aerial photographs in the excellent guide-book that I realise that what I took to be an inner and outer ring are actually inner and outer shells joined on

the rear or Orwell side. The moat is mostly on the landward side.
The outer aspect is almost without opening: the doors and windows
face mostly inwards. The shell-like structure means that many of
the rooms have curved walls and arched corridors that gently curl
away from you around bends. The fort is built of innumerable
bricks, each placed one by one to create smooth curves and
pyramidal angles. It was built by and for tough men, when health
and safety wasn't such a public responsibility – as testified by a
notice "Ancient Monuments can be Dangerous. Please take care".

There is plenty to stir the fancy in Landguard Fort: walking down
an unlit curved corridor, I go as far as I dare (my imagination firing
on all cylinders) glancing back nervously at the lit doorway, until
the curve takes it from sight. I carry on, toe tapping against the
wall to help me round the bend, for an eternity (just a
microsecond), before my nerve fails and I turn back to the light.

Back in the light of day, from the first floor, particularly from the
Harwich Bastion, there are spectacular views; you can see the two
Martello Towers over on the Harwich side, and the site of the
Dooley fort up the estuary in what is now the docks, as well as
Hangar no 1, which was part of the flying boat experimental station
– in fact that whole area was given over to military huts and mining
equipment, as well as HMS Beehive. The Army, Navy, and RAF all
had a presence here: in World War I there were over 30,000 military

personnel in Felixstowe. To the left are the searchlight boxes that fired beams of light horizontally across the water for night firing and Darrell's Battery; to the right, buildings that housed the submarine mining establishment. I take in the vastness of the port and watch for a while the harbour activity, gulls wheeling overhead and the under-mining work being done by rabbits in the far bank. The gun placements on this battlement (where steel rings are a reminder of the guns that used to swing about spitting fire) have some of the best views from the Fort - I guess it was this commanding position which caused the guns to be placed here.

In one room, steel lined and made of granite to render it bombproof, is a huge cannon. Here I come across a small detail of volunteers. The fort has a four-year painting cycle to resist the elements, tours to be guided, repairs to be done, and each group of volunteers has their own specific task – guides, painters, carpenters and dust-busters. It's this army of enthusiasts that keeps the place together.

There are all kinds of things to look at; the windowless room for anti-aircraft operations during the Second World War, where you imagine men bending over the large plotting table; the wireless room; a display about Martello Towers; a video room; the magazine, where the men had to remove their boots and uniforms and wear special cotton pocket-less overalls, as anything like the nails on the bottom of hobnail boots could have created a spark which would cause an explosion. The re-creation of the shoemakers shop is very evocative, a poignant reminder of ordinary everyday tasks. Sets of worn shoes and metal lasts, each shaped to the contours of a particular foot sit on a shelf. You can't look at the empty worn boots without wondering what happened to the feet that wore them. A reconstruction of a bedroom is bleak - a grey army blanket over a cot - despite a table set with decanters and pewter mugs, and the carpet on the floor, it feels far from luxurious. It is though, in comparison to the reconstruction of a Victorian barrack room from the late 19th century, when *better sanitary arrangements, improved ventilation and a space allowance of at least 600 cubic feet per man*" were just some of the innovations. It is chilly enough in there in the daytime, but hard to imagine anyone enduring the conditions when there weren't enough beds to go around and many had to sleep on the floor, with short rations, freezing cold and waiting for pay. No wonder there was once a mutiny.

What I enjoy most is wandering around, finding my own everyday ghosts of past inhabitants in the traces of use. The upper rooms are flooded with sunlight across their wooden floors, so much warmer than the ground floor. This is where the officers lived, and there are shelves, cupboards and remarkably small fireplaces with empty grates. Downstairs there are deserted washrooms with moulded gullies to draw water away, gaps where pipes once flowed, and traces of coats of different coloured paint worn through the layers to reveal brick beneath. In one room there's even a faint remainder of stencilled floral decoration, an attempt to domesticate a harsh environment. These things are evidence of the everyday activities that made up the life of the place for so long. The guide book sums up the soldiers' experience brilliantly: "*Life for the garrison soldier was a mixture of routine and boredom punctuated by occasional excitement.*"

I leave the Fort and go round to the Viewing Point car park to get a bite of lunch from the Crow's Nest wagon (very popular with ship spotters and walkers alike), and watch the harbour for a while. There's a dredger at work again and small flurries of activity, but it's

obviously a lull between arrivals or departures of the big cargo containers and only a solitary pilot boat chugs back to harbour after seeing off a much larger vessel. This part of the port is apparently due for redevelopment, with a new Landguard Visitors Centre and improved Foot Ferry berth planned.

The military history of Landguard doesn't end with the fort: there are remains of over three hundred and eighty military installations on the Landguard Peninsula. Some of these are in evidence on the windswept spaces of the Nature Reserve. Concrete structures dot the landscape, circles, cubes and steps, like megalithic sites or ancient Aztec tombs in miniature. I enter the Nature Reserve past a board belonging to the Landguard Bird Observatory, which states that Brent geese, a Pallas warbler and a lesser whitethroat had been spotted over Landguard today, I spot a magpie and a pigeon. I head across to the Rangers Cottage, where I'd arranged to meet Sarah Wynne, the current incumbent of the Ranger's post.

The Ranger's Cottage looks like an ordinary modern bungalow, but is in fact one of the earliest extant examples of cavity wall building, designed by Peter Bruff in about 1880. It was damaged by mortar shells during firing practice in the 1940s or 50s. It's a very peaceful spot. The only sounds above the backing track of breaking waves are a blackbird's alarm call, a barking dog, and the constant hum of the port. As your ear gets tuned in you hear an alarm sound from the port (a truck reversing?) and the sudden outbreak of chatter and squabbling interspersed with a whispering call as a flock of starlings swoop in to perch on a dock tower. The Reserve's resident pair of magpies is pecking at the ground alongside a trio of rabbits. Sarah tells me that there aren't many predators here, the odd weasel, an old vixen who died recently, but it looks as though another fox might have moved into the territory. There are kestrels, sparrow hawks and peregrines. Ringed plovers and oystercatchers nest on the shingle, little terns used to nest here too, but haven't for many years, though efforts are being made to create secluded spots to lure them back.

Camden, who wrote before the first fort was erected on Landguard described it as a shore that was "*well defended by a vast ridge two miles long out at sea,*

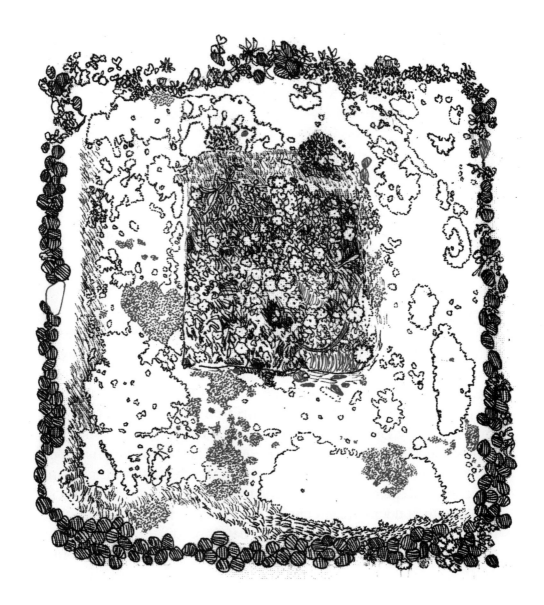

called Langerston, not without great danger and terror to mariners. 'Tis however of use to fishermen for drying of their fish, and does in a manner fence the spacious harbour of Orwell". More evidence of the constant shift in the shape of the land. The shingle at this end of the point is unstable, and consequently there are different varieties of plants from those on the shingle behind the sea wall at the Common end. Here lines of sea kale give way to swathes of yellow horned-poppy and bands of sea peas, as different plants find the strip of land most suitable for them. The yellow horned-poppy has seed heads of up to 30cm long, possibly the longest of any British wildflower, and waxy feeling flowers and leaves to combat dehydration. There's sea holly too, which is good for butterflies, and endless tiny sedums which store water in tiny pouches, with pale snails threading their way through. There's also sea spurge, a declining species, which prefers the shifting shingle to the stable sort. We scrutinise a patch of ground where Sarah saw some stinking goosefoot recently, but it has gone underground

for winter.

The landscape looks pretty empty – there are unruly tufts of brambles at this end, which apparently will have to be removed because they threaten the environment of some of the tiny rare wildflowers. Elsewhere at the Common end the blackberry bushes will be left, as they provide food and nesting habitat for songbirds. As you get your eye in to the subtleties of the landscape you notice a series of shallow ridges and troughs, the brighter green mosses in the damper bottom of the trough and a silver lichen on the ridges. There are small concrete squares, remnants of who knows what long-forgotten military purpose, which now bound miniature self-contained worlds of plant and insect life. Life and death go on: we walk past rotting corpses of dead rabbits – victims, Sarah says, of last summer's drought - and shells on the shingle where resourceful gulls have flown over the land and dropped shellfish to break them open.

Sarah shows me the lying sleepers of a railway line arching out to the sea – maybe this was the line that was used to carry the mines which were set out on the channel bed. The wood is knotted and sea-worn, the concrete that surrounds it worn back like sandstone to reveal the pebbles it contains standing out like newly revealed fossils.

Landguard Common is a mecca for dog walkers, with everything from bernese mountain dogs to pekinese. One woman I talk to says that she walks there every day with her dog, come rain or shine, so gets to see the Common changing with the seasons, observing the minute shifts as plants come out, come into flower and die away at the end of the season.

Thursday

Thursday dawns bright and clear. Given that it's December, I've been very lucky with the weather all week, no rain and all days but one sunny and bright. As I cycle into Felixstowe Ferry I see thirty or so walkers starting off along the sea wall towards Felixstowe, silhouetted against the sky. Presumably these are people going on the Health Walk that I'd seen advertised at the Tourist Information Office. I've decided to do walk number 2 from the *Walking Around Felixstowe* booklet, a good seven mile hike that overlaps the Martello Coast Path on the last section, and begins at Felixstowe Ferry.

I start my walk by the village sign for Felixstowe Ferry, opposite some beautiful wooden beach bungalows, one with the chimney decorated with dragon-like scales and a "bird" perched on a post on the roof. The sign could exemplify what makes good site-specific art work. It depicts two boats (a sailing boat and perhaps an old ferry boat) crossing on the waves in front of a Martello Tower, itself silhouetted against the rays of the setting sun. There is continuity to the long tradition of village signs in East Anglia, and in its demonstration of the skills of the blacksmith craft. The design is simple, effective and pleasing. The sign was designed by Barrie White, and the ironwork done by the Kirton blacksmith, Alex Jacobs.

From here a concrete path leads away parallel with the River

Deben, before disappearing around a bend. As I sit writing this, a bird, larger than a pigeon, swoops along the line of the path, barely eight inches away from me. It happens so fast I don't get a good look at it, just an impression of golden buff undercarriage and a slightly black speckled back.

I walk along to the melodic clinking of halyards against a mast. There is the distinctive silhouette of a peewit high overhead. Once past the houses and hedges the path opens out on the right to views across the mudflats of boats, the river and Bawdsey itself. Bawdsey Manor, one of the big houses hereabouts, was the site of secret research in WWII, important in the development of radar. RAF personnel used to take the Ferry across and bus into Felixstowe for rest and relaxation.

It's a beautiful day to be out walking, one of those mornings when all is right with the world. I watch the constant play of light on water, and the unceasing activity of the shore birds - the nominative call of the peewit adding to the view of it overhead. The retreating tide makes fascinating patterns in the estuary mud as ox-bowing sluices drain paths back towards the parent water. The boats moored here are older, and have a more lived in feel. There is one bleached and stranded on its side on a mud bank, and, lifting my eyes to the horizon, I see many others in a similar state stretching away into the distance; in their silver-grey decay, with the occasional rib exposed, they make me think of an elephants' graveyard.

Next I come upon a surprising hippopotamus installation: a jetty and boat dotted around with drawings and sculptures of hippos, divers' heads peering out from the mud, hands reaching for ladders.

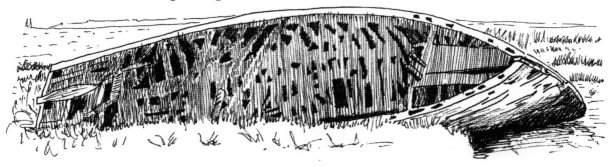

Faces peer through boat windows back at me. It is all, as the signs inform me, just "pottering about".

I walk on to a bend in the path, and there is another sign, this one somewhat ambiguous, telling me that there is a right of way, but basically warning me off the golf course, at pain of injury. I turn right to safety, following the river's course. There's a solitary cottage ahead on my left in the middle of an

archetypal Suffolk landscape, flat in the foreground, with trees and water, a big sky and rolling at the edges. It feels a bit like walking in a Constable painting. It is striking how one painter can dominate our perception of a landscape.

A flight of geese is following the river inland, the distinctive black fronts and white bums of Brent geese travelling in arrow head formation. There are hovers of smaller birds closer to, rising up in twos and threes and piping like skylarks. The sound of wind

in my ears is punctuated by distant shots. I can see the towers of the BT headquarters way off, but otherwise it's an entirely rural view; utterly charming, with a variety of visual stimuli and sounds, play of light and man-made features. I think of the continuity of use of this fertile land; of Saxons stealing in their boats up to Sutton Hoo. There is evidence of a Saxon presence in Felixstowe, though not as dramatic as it's famous neighbour. A bronze lion broach, bronze combs and a bone disc were dug up, some artefacts are in the museum at Ipswich, some went to the British Museum in London.

A pair of walkers come towards me, binoculars in hand, some of the few I'm to see for the rest of the walk. More geese go over, this time with black necks, a white flash and grey backs. Canadas, I think. From my vantage point on the high bank I have excellent views, and see the Kings Fleet cutting away from the main river at right angles on my left. This river is so named because it is believed that Edward the Third kept a fleet of ships there in 1338, in preparation for an invasion of France. This is my last view of the Fleet for a while, as I descend some steps down the bank and follow a broad track cutting between farmland and the river itself, hidden by banks, willows and rushes.

I'm intrigued by a number of large white blobs in a field up ahead on the right. They're the wrong shape for sheep, and somehow they're too white. As I get closer thirty or forty heads shoot up in the air simultaneously and reveal themselves to be swans grazing on the newly germinated crop. I've never seen such a large group on land before. In the next field, on the other side of the track, there are some sheep. Most of them have speckled faces and bad-hair-day topknots, but two have the look typical of neater, meatier and more compact Poll Suffolk. It's silly, I know, but for some reason it seems very fitting and pleasing to see Suffolk sheep in Suffolk!

There's a great sense of peace about the place and, in fact, very few people around. A solitary tractor goes by, the driver nodding in greeting, and I turn uphill between hedges, away from the river. The land is productive here, winter wheat on one side and a field

of kale on the other. There is a smell of wood smoke as I crest the rise, and glancing across I see the farmhouse on my left. Looking behind me through a gap in the hedge to the right, I can see right the way back along the path I've walked, all the way to Felixstowe Ferry, taking in the Martello Tower and the tips of Bawdsey Manor through the pines. On past another farmhouse, this one with a handsome portico, and brick stabling given a new lease of life as a garage. I can smell pigs, but can't see any, until up over the next rise there is a field of maybe fifty of them. I seem to have reached the highest point of the walk, the land rolling away back towards the Deben, in the distance is a water tower (do they have to irrigate the farmland?) and a small lake. Now, for the first time since

leaving the road I can hear the hum of traffic; a constant interchange between Ipswich and Felixstowe. A lot of the cargo from the port finds itself travelling on the backs of lorries along this route, and onwards all across England.

I descend again to a curious dip, where a belt of trees shelters dual parallel brooks, their banks carefully maintained and built up high. Emerging on the other side I see on my left an unusually rectangular pond. All around me is arable land, the soil red and sandy-silty. Up another gentle hill and I look across and realise that

I'm on a level with Felixstowe Ferry and the coast, though it feels as if I must have climbed higher. I guess the land actually dips down and then up again, which is sobering when you think what might happen here if sea levels were to rise.

Arable yields to grazing, with the character of an estate parkland. Massive oaks dominate the fields, before giving way to a belt of straighter poplars which guard another stream though woodland. I put up partridge and pigeon as I climb a stile into the small copse. Across a wooden bridge over the gurgling stream and back out onto arable land. Walking uphill the traffic sounds seem louder and I

turn towards the sound; just before it's hidden by a belt of trees I see – a world away – a constant stream of traffic pouring oblivious and relentless in both directions. The belt of trees also conceals an ancient pond, and behind it a mellow Suffolk brick, timber and tile house. My arrival surprises a gaggle of moorhens and a pair of mallard, whose startled flight across the water in turn startles me.

One house I walk by has a notice on the gateway *"Grade 1 and 2 Farmland, Environmentally sensitive and bordering AONB. Potential site for over 1,620 homes."* I guess the countryside I've been walking over could be swallowed up, and one day Ipswich and Felixstowe will join.

Following instructions in the book, I turn right off Gulpher Road along the first footpath I come to, past a kestrel hovering above the undergrowth lining a drainage channel. My path doesn't read like the description in the book, which said I should be going up hill. Maybe I've taken a wrong turn? Possibly a mis-direction in the book and it should have said the second footpath on the right off Gulpher Road. I carry on, to see where it takes me. Sometimes it feels good to go off the map! My diversion turns out to be short and made more than worthwhile by a colony of long-tailed tits who accompany me along the tree-lined path. I get to the top of a rise, and there is what must be the path I should have taken coming up the hill to my left. On my right there is some sort of public space,

and I can hear the whiney buzz of model aeroplanes. Traffic noises recede behind me, and up ahead I see the outskirts of Felixstowe: farmland stretches away from me on the left, neat housing on the right. Skirting around the edge of the town on Ferry Road I walk past a modern house with an imaginative and original wall drawing on one side. In the field on the other side of the road the ground is thick with a huge flock of pigeons. A big mistle thrush sits in a garden tree top, looking down her beak at me.

I cross the main road, which I biked up earlier on my way to Felixstowe Ferry, to a patch of grass near the golf course club house. Planted in the expanse of grass are a number of pine trees, which form the second part of Simon Read's artwork, "To Forgotten Fleets" which I saw on the Martello Coast Path on Monday. The trees, scots pine, form an open triangle at points of alignments to the buoyage for the approaches to Felixstowe and Woodbridge Haven. The trees appeared stunted, and even a little bent by the onshore winds – one in particular, nearest to houses overlooking the trees appears to have suffered a little "pruning" to its main growth stem. Underneath the trees are metal posts bearing photos of boat drawings carved into tree bark. These were found by the artist at nearby Butley Clumps, an 18th Century plantation, and are all of local beach boats, trawlers and trading vessels. The drawings are beautiful: blurred and distorted as the tree, the drawing surface, has grown and changed over time.

I go down some steps to the sea shore. The sea is again showing the world a different mood, calm and blue with hardly a white top in sight. There are sea birds malingering on the shingle, no doubt keeping out of the cold wind. The warm orange brown pebbles glow intensely against the blue sky. On the golf course there are changes too, with groups of people standing and walking about purposefully. Felixstowe Golf Club was established in 1880, on only the fifth course to be built in England. Perhaps the most famous member was the right Honourable Arthur Balfour, later Prime Minister, who was captain of the Golf Club in 1889. I pass Martello Tower

'T" again, which is looking decidedly more cheerful in the sunshine, apparently it was once used as the golf club house.

I walk briskly on to Felixstowe Ferry, hoping to reach the café there in time for a late lunch. I'd been told that they do a really good fish and chips, and feel that I've earned it after my long walk. I'm in luck. Despite being a late Thursday in December, the café is two thirds full with customers young and old – it must get absolutely packed in the summer season – apparently clever people park at the Cliff Top parking and walk down. I sit at a table by the long wall of windows, bathed in sunshine. Another wall is adorned with maps and newspaper clippings, sea pictures and local pictures. On a third wall there are pictures of fish, and nets hung with plastic crabs, lobster and cuttle fish, as well as vitrines of model boats.

After lunch I have a look around Felixstowe Ferry before heading back into town. There are two shops selling fresh fish, caught by the fleet which still fishes out of the harbour here. I talk to one fisherman who is repairing a boat, who says that there are plenty of fish out there, at this time of year mostly cod. In summer they get Dover sole, bass and lobster. Some of the fish they sell locally, but much gets put on a boat and sold in Holland or Belgium.

One of the things I like most about Felixstowe Ferry is the beach bungalows of all different shapes and sizes, many customised by

imaginative owners. There's also the jetty, with a ferry across to Bawdsey in the summer, and, on the side of one of the beach huts, a notice board with photos and articles about local people and the village. There seems to be a strong feeling of community here.

Friday

It's nearing the end of my week in Felixstowe, and the day starts with my now routine breakfast at the Elizabeth Orwell.

The hotel dining room is quite ornate, with beautiful chandeliers, moulded ceilings and gold pillars. It is furnished with Regency style chairs and decorated in cream and red. The walls are hung with paintings in ornate gold frames; some ubiquitously gloomy portraits, but a few pretty beach scenes and seascapes, as well as still lifes of fruit in keeping with the dining room's purpose. The tables are laid with white starched cloths, fanned napkins, sparkling glass and silverware. It's beautifully done, though feels quite heavy to me, I suppose it's a recreation of the Edwardian/late Victorian style of the hotel's heyday. The service is very attentive, and the breakfasts excellent!

Last night it rained for the first time this week, and the morning starts grey and misty. I set off on the bike towards Trimley Marshes, a bird reserve run by the Suffolk Wildlife Trust on the banks of the River

Orwell, just upstream from the Port of Felixstowe. I have an interesting journey. First through Felixstowe suburbs, following cycle route 5, where I see a different side of the town to the coastal housing alongside the Martello Coast Path. Then in towards the business end of the docks, which employ so many Felixstowe residents. Here there's a lot more heavy traffic, including all the lorries heading towards or away from the port. Finally I turn onto Fagbury Road, where cycling along on my bike I am dwarfed by a long line of huge lorries. Then I leave the road, go through a gate, across the railway line, through two more gates and into a narrow copse. I lock the bike by the last gate, as the path looked unsuitable for bikes. Carrying on on foot, I walk along with a belt of trees on one side and the port on the other. Seeing it from this end I realise how huge it actually is. It is, of course, the major employer in Felixstowe, some say the town would have died without it, and it also contributes support to various local projects and good causes. It contributes also to the interest of the area; a lot of people are drawn to the Viewing Point to see the ships come and go. However, I've also come across a certain amount of feeling that the port dominates the town too much, and cynicism that the port was allowed to

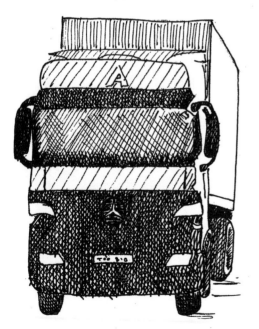

knock down and build over sites of historic interest, as well as Sites of Special Scientific interest. Trimley Marshes, I've been told, was set up in compensation for habitat lost nearer the mouth of the estuary when the port expanded.

I walk on up Fagbury Cliffs – not as imposing as the name suggests - a rise in the ground with seating and a clear view out over the workings of the Port. Then the path turns away from the Port and the River Orwell, across beautiful farmland. The sun is by now coming out, and I walk down what must be an ancient track, lined on both sides by centuries old oak trees. The path turns at right angles again, bordered by trees on one side, and farmland on the other, taking the line of an old road towards the Reserve. I start to wish that I'd kept the bike with me, as there was only one short stretch at the beginning where I'd have had to push it. There are a few pigeons and crows scattered in the fields, but little other evidence of bird life. Then, just before the entrance to the Reserve, there's a kestrel hovering and further away in the distance a heron standing guard over a ditch. Minutes into the reserve, still walking the line of the old road with trees on either side now, a green woodpecker swoops by me, quick as a flash, but easily identifiable from it's red cap and vivid yellow-green rump. The call is very distinctive too, an insistent "pæuu. pæuu". I meet a man walking away from the Reserve, bristling with binoculars and camera lenses. We stop and chat, and he tells me that he's seen pintail ducks, avocet, pochard and red-crested pochard. I'm excited, as I've never seen avocet, with their long legs and upward curving beaks. The road opens out, and there again on the left are the docks. I don't know how many miles I've walked, but they've been there all the time behind the

trees. That, however, is the last sight of them, as the track bends again to follow the line of the River Orwell upstream. I leave the proper path and climb onto the high bank to get a view of the river. There's a sailing boat skimming it's way up towards Ipswich, and little egrets and ringed plover down by the river's edge.

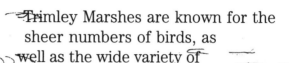

Trimley Marshes are known for the sheer numbers of birds, as well as the wide variety of species that can be found on the wetlands. It's a man-made habitat, created in 1990 from former arable land. There are lagoons, islands, wetland meadows, reedbeds, networks of dykes and of course the estuary margins. Large parts of the land making up the Reserve are managed for the benefit of the wildlife, with human visitor access restricted. There is, however, a number of strategically placed hides, with excellent views across the wetlands, and a visitors centre (which is unfortunately closed today).

I settle into a hide overlooking a lagoon, and get my binoculars out. I could see shoveler, shelduck, gadwall, coots and Brent geese, but alas, no avocet. I am surprised though, at the large numbers of birds present.

After a while, I retrace my steps back to the bike. Apparently a train is expected into the docks, visible along the tracks, but

I am waved across by some workmen who hold the gates open for me. The queue of lorries on Fagbury Road has gone down. Instead of retracing my route into town, I skirt around the edge of the Port down to Landguard, where I had an appointment to visit the Museum.

I am shown around by Sue Tod, archivist and a member of the Felixstowe History and Museum Society, a group of volunteers inaugurated in 1978 with the aim of opening a museum. The Museum is housed in the former Sub-marine Mining Establishment building, constructed by the Royal Engineers in 1878 to house and store sub-marine mines. The mines were for harbour defence. I must clarify that they were not mines to blow up submarines (as I initially understood it, thinking, "Wow, I didn't know they had submarines that early!"), but mines that were set underwater (sub-marine not submarine). The building was handed over to the Navy in 1905, then around about 1910 actual submarine vessels came into operation and sub-marine mines were obsolete. Later on, the Army took over the building as stores and offices, and finally it was occupied until 1976 by the Ministry of Works. It was left empty for three or so years until the Society negotiated for the building in 1979, by which time it was in a pretty derelict state. However, with hard work from the volunteers the first room of the Museum opened to the public in 1982. Now every inch of the building is in use, and filled to overflowing with artefacts relating to the history of the area. It continues to this day as an independently run museum, staffed and managed entirely through the hard work and enthusiasm of the Society members, and reliant upon donations for new material and support. The Museum in season has special "Behind the Scenes" days, and also there are a number of activities, such as knot-tying demonstrations all done by volunteers.

One example of the donations, shown to me by Sue, was an attractive painting of Felixstowe, showing Martello Tower 'P' and a bell tent, from the 1920s. Apparently, on one 'red letter day', a couple walked in and said that it had been hanging in their front parlour somewhere in Romford, and would the Museum like it?

Most of the collection is from the 19th and early 20th Centuries, but there are a few things which are much older - such as Roman artefacts or, older still, a Neolithic flint knife, which was found on a Trimley farm. The collection is wide-ranging: there is a photographic archive, including many photos from the 1953 floods; maps; collections reflecting the town's historic intertwining with all

three of the armed forces; artefacts (but no records) from St Audry's Asylum; a whole roomful of items forming a paddle steamer exhibit, several loaned by the Paddle Steamer Preservation Society (including a model of the paddle steamer, La Marguerite, which apparently lots of the kids who visit think is the Titanic); an archaeology room and a display of a 1914 grocer's shop, with a huge cabinet taken from a local shop, which Society members were told they could have if they could get it out.

Things that catch my eye in particular are a 1938 delivery van, cheek by jowl with some cherubs rescued from the demolition of the Felixstowe Playhouse and a large-scale model of the Red Baron aeroplane. In the Aircraft Room are albums of photographs taken from a World War I plane, and a poster of the Westminster Abbey Battle of Britain window, which glows with jewel-like colours. The range of models, of planes and ships, all made by volunteers is truly impressive. I also enjoy the archaeology display, largely devoted to the story of Thomas Mariner Felgate's excavation of the Old Hall at Walton. Felgate, who had served in all three services in World War I started the excavation, but when funding ran out in the 1960s his finds were left in a shed on site, which was locked up and left. It

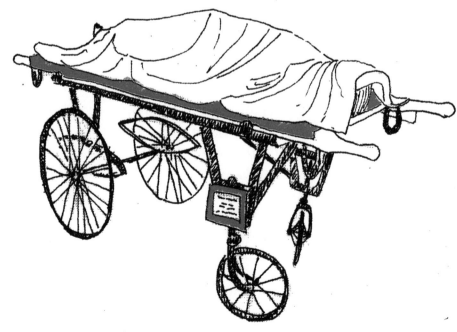

wasn't opened again until 1997, when it was discovered intact, and the display in the Museum recreates the shed as it was on the day it was reopened. There's a beautiful drawing by Betty Holford-Smith, who was an art teacher at Felixstowe College, a design for the Old Felixstowe sign. I am struck by a pair of panoramic photographs showing areas I had walked and cycled around earlier, before the docks were extended. There's a fascinating hand-drawn map of the Landguard Peninsula, showing just how the coast has changed in the last two hundred or so years; a display of cannon balls, the stocks and whipping post from Walton, which all too easily project into the imagination how they would have been used. There is also a very moving collection of the inscriptions from the graveyard on Landguard Peninsula, copied and saved before it was drowned by the sea.

Friday night is party night, or at least my big night out. I had a seat reserved for the Big Band Concert at the Spa Pavilion, with the Syd Lawrence Orchestra. There has been a theatre on this site since 1905, and before that there was a massive wrought iron bandstand with space for 30 musicians and seating for up to 400 concert goers. The site was chosen not only for its proximity to the sea, but also to the Spa waters, which were reputedly anti-dyspeptic, anti-gout and *"a capital medicine for those suffering from nervous prostrations, depression and overwork"*. The theatre predates the gardens, which were opened to much pomp by the Mayor of London in 1928.

I arrive at the Spa Pavilion early, to have a meal in the restaurant before the performance. The restaurant has windows all the length of one long side, and fine views of the sea and passing ships. At night the sea is in darkness, but you can see the occasional ship's lights off in the distance, and the pretty multi-coloured lights of the promenade.

Inside the auditorium the stage looks inviting with soft pinks and blues. The Spa Pavilion plays a strong role in promoting local theatre, giving up a big chunk of its calendar to local theatre groups, and also hosting Felixstowe's Annual Drama Festival. Tonight is music night, a mostly brass line-up delivering an essentially American sound, with a smoothly professional delivery which is well received by the two-thirds full house. It wasn't my cup of tea but nevertheless a skilful and authentic experience.

119

Saturday

My last morning in Felixstowe dawns bright but very cold, made even colder by a brisk northerly wind. My first destination of the day is the Landguard Bird Observatory, where I'd arranged to meet Nigel from the Observatory and Sarah, the Landguard Ranger. Nigel has been watching and netting birds at the Observatory for a very long time, so has built up a sense of the changing patterns in wildlife that comes with time. Experts at the observatory catch birds in a Heligoland net, ring them, or take note of the rings they are already wearing, record numbers and then release them. The net is a kind of giant funnel, originally developed over a hundred years ago in the Baltic states, to catch birds like fieldfares, blackbirds and redwings to salt down and eat. Now they provide a way of being able to catch the birds without harming them so that they can be ringed, which builds up information about bird populations and movements. It also gives information about birds' life spans – one turnstone found this year was one that had originally been ringed in 1992. From ringing surveys, we now know that most British turnstones (or, rather, turnstones that overwinter in Britain) come from Greenland and Canada and they can live for up to twenty years.

As well as ringing birds, the Observatory volunteers also set moth traps for nine months of the year, and record the fluctuations of moth numbers. Over the twenty years of surveying this has produced some surprising results, including finding species not commonly found outside Africa. Bird numbers are of course linked to moth numbers, as moths and caterpillars are an important food source for many varieties of bird. Some of the moth species found on Landguard Point are red data book species – this could be due to the vegetated shingle, which is a rare habitat. Most shingle isn't vegetated, but Suffolk has a significant percentage of the UK's vegetated shingle, and Landguard supplies some of that. The rare habitat means that you get rare plants, which in turn means that you get rare moths. In a way, the moths are as site specific to the habitat as the plants are. The vegetated shingle on Landguard is, however, under threat - this time from sand which is washing down from the town beaches. Spending time at Landguard you realise that even the land migrates – pebbles have been found here that have come from Northern Europe.

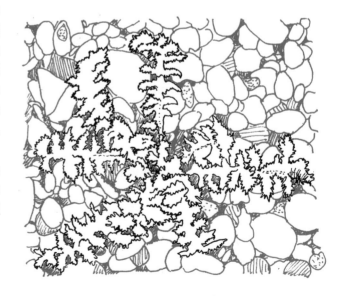

We talk a bit about the potential effects of climate change on wildlife, and Nigel

says that recent years have shown
a significant decline in the number
of birds recorded, and of moths
trapped. This year has been the worst
ever, with a serious downturn in the
numbers of migrating species, such as
starlings counted. Brent geese have
been coming in shockingly smaller
numbers, too. In previous years, the
Observatory recorded counts of up to 40,000
per day, whereas this winter there have only
been two counts which have got to over 1,000.
(Sarah had a particularly good description for
recognising a Brent goose in flight – a cross between a mallard
and a Tornado!). Not all the changes can be put down to climate
change – for example birds that used to be seen regularly on
Landguard could have disappeared because they are being fed in
gardens in town. Also fewer blackbirds are migrating from the
continent to overwinter, but again, this could be because affluence
and bird awareness in human populations has increased – if people
are supplying plentiful amounts of quality food it becomes less
important for the birds to migrate somewhere else to escape the
cold. The docks also affect bird behaviour. For example a lot of
birds migrate at night, and they can be attracted by the dock lights
– Felixstowe is "lit up like a mushroom", which I guess acts as a
kind of navigational aid. Also the dock warehouse roofs have been

providing nesting sites for lesser black-backed gulls over the last twenty years. You get regional variations too – Mediterranean gulls, which are a rare sight in large parts of the UK, are quite common at Landguard.

At Landguard they also do their bit to help the bird populations get through the winter. Sarah and I help do a bit of pre-Christmas tree dressing – pushing apples onto twigs and branches to keep the local blackbirds happy. It's not just the birds which like the apples: the rabbits (there are hundreds on the Landguard Peninsula) love apples too, and I notice rabbit damage on some of the trees at head height – acrobatic rabbits!

Apparently all the trees on this part of the Peninsula were planted by the military to help camouflage the buildings.

Nigel gives me an explanation as to why the sea is a different colour here in Felixstowe to that I'm used to in the West – apparently it's because the sea just here has a very shallow coastal margin, and there is a lot of erosion, so the water has a lot of sediment in it. This means, he says, you don't get to see whales or dolphins around here, but you do get porpoises, which, like cormorants, hunt by feel!

The change in weather with an intensifying of the cold, compared to earlier in the week, has brought more birds inland. This morning watchers have already seen great northern divers and eider. There is a group of birdwatchers, with an impressive collection of binoculars between them, looking out from a hide (part of an old military lookout, perhaps) over the sea. Their sightings for that day are recorded on the Bird Observatory website, and also provide useful data about bird numbers and migration. Species recorded in the week I'd been in Felixstowe included: long-tailed ducks; eider; common scoter; gadwall; little egret; great northern diver; red-throated diver; black-throated diver; Brent geese; white-fronted geese; gannets;

Mediterranean gulls; lesser redpoll; brambling; linnets and skylark. The work done by these volunteers is another example of the kind of passion for a particular subject that I've come across so often in my week in Felixstowe, where people dedicate large amounts of their time and effort to something they believe is important.

I go back up through the town, stopping to look at St Andrew's Church – an example of twentieth century ecclesiastical architecture. I am pleasantly surprised by it, given that it's made

out of reinforced concrete, and so different to other buildings around it, I find its simple lines and pleasing proportions impressive. There are turreted towers with narrow slit windows that give it a rather castle-like feel. The architect was Hilda Mason, and it was built in the early 1930s. The glass is mostly plain, as indeed is the interior decoration, though this just intensifies the colours of the one stained glass window above the altar. Unfortunately, I'm told, the steel reinforcing inside the concrete is corroding, which is causing chunks of concrete to crumble away.

For my final walk I decide to do Walk no.1 from *Walking around Felixstowe*. This starts from what is known locally as "The Grove" – apparently it's a rarity as there is otherwise little deciduous woodland in the neighbourhood. There is a mixture of oak, sycamore, ash and hawthorn and also some truly huge holly trees, which I think are slow growing, so they've obviously been there for a while. I manage to get the path wrong again, obviously taking a fork too early, and so miss out on the marshes, though I do come out onto the playing fields, so at least get to the right place. There are lots of people out walking dogs, practising fishing casts, playing with the kids or flying model planes. One of the latter seems to twist vertically downwards in a nosedive right above my head, before swooping up and away.

I emerge from the playing field onto a muddy lane, with a field of rich red-brown, newly ploughed furrows on the other side. The next field along has winter wheat already germinating. Here where town meets countryside there's a noticeable contrast in the housing; the newer estates, built in the late 20th century jostle up against older single houses from the area's agricultural past. I turn in past some allotments off to the right. There are lots of sheds, netting and birdscarers, but not much veg in sight at this time of year, and surprisingly few people, given that it's a Saturday. At the end of the path there's another reminder of Felixstowe's military past in the form of a concrete bunker. Then out onto the road and I go past a small, old schoolhouse, with a lantern on the roof which I'm beginning to recognise as typical of the architectural vernacular of the area. The afternoon, which had turned sunny, is beginning to fade towards evening light. I round a bend

and glimpse a Martello Tower in the distance, half hidden by trees and a panoramic view of the golf course, the sea and Bawdsey behind. There's a forest of masts glinting in the dying sun at Felixstowe Ferry, and a hint of dusk on the calm sea. The bungalows that line this road, with names like Deben Retreat, have fantastic views of the sea and estuary. Some of the tidy gardens, with vigorously pollarded trees, still have arum lilies in flower.

I cross the road and descend the steps beside the Armada Beacon. Even though it's only half past three the Beacon is silhouetted against a pink hued sky. I cross into the Area of Outstanding Natural Beauty and see the sea turning silver in the evening light. I walk along the sea wall in the direction of town. Somewhere off to my left under the sea are the remains of Walton Castle – a Roman Fort - one of the "forts of the Saxon shore". The foundations were measured in 1740, and found to be 187 yards in length. Stones from the castle were used to pave footpaths around Old Felixstowe. Then as the shape of the coast changed the remains of the fort were swallowed by the sea – though many people I've spoken to say that they're still visible at exceptionally low tides. On the heights above me on the right is the site of Brackenbury Fort. I

climb some steep steps up the cliff and across the road at the top, which brings me out roughly where the Brackenbury Barracks would have been. During World War II a Ukrainian Bomb Disposal Unit was stationed at Brackenbury. Many of them stayed on after the war, clearing up the bombs that were left all along the East coast, and some of them are buried in Felixstowe cemetery.

The route then follows a series of footpaths which bisect the housing, sometimes channelled between high fences, sometimes affording intimate views of houses and gardens. It opens out by the Church of St Peter and St Paul at Old Felixstowe. This is a fascinating building, dating from around the 14th century, with irregular patterns of brick and stone work, including septaria, a local soft stone which was quarried near Cobbolds Point. It is locked on this occasion, so I am limited to admiring the beautifully clipped yews, the squat tower and the handsome lychgate.

Opposite the church is the sign for Old Felixstowe Village. It was created in 1979 to commemorate the Diamond Jubilee of the Old Felixstowe Women's Institute. It was designed by Mrs. Joan Meredith, then president of the Old Felixstowe WI, carved by Jim Norman from English oak, and the ironwork was forged by Alex Jacobs at the nearby Kirton smithy. The sign depicts a roman arch (for the Roman settlement in the area) a monk of the priory that was in evidence during the reign of Edward III, and a ship of his navy.

I go back along more suburban streets to where I'd left the bike at the Grove. I just have time to return the bike before I catch my train. The train is on time, and not crowded. It feels as though I am venturing out into another world after my week in Felixstowe. On the train I reflect back upon my week, and the character of the town I have just left.

The thing that stands out as the unifying force behind all the different facets to Felixstowe – the military history, the wildlife, the boom days as a seaside resort, its attraction to today's visitors, and the contemporary dominance of the docks – is, of course, the sea. The sea brings in trade through the port. Without the sea it could hardly be a seaside resort. The sea brought attack (or the threat of attack) by Romans, Saxons, Dutch, French and Germans. Felixstowe's position on the coast between two major inland waterways gave it national strategic importance. It was an ironically short gap of years between the visit by the Empress of Germany (grand-daughter-in-law to Queen Victoria) which is given so much credit in establishing Felixstowe as a fashionable resort, and the wave of military expansion in the town in preparation for German attack by air and sea. The sea has been and is a source of wealth to the local economy – not just through the port and the tourist industry, but also through the boat yards and fishing industry. The sea continues to attract visitors today, both on holiday and on day trips from nearby towns. It brings the real and present threat of erosion, which, if unchecked, could take chunks of the town away; and the threat of obliteration if climate change causes sea levels to rise as predicted. It is the proximity to the sea that creates the environment for the rare and important vegetated shingle and the plants and moths that thrive here. More peaceful migrants than the Danes and Romans come across the sea to Felixstowe too, turnstones, starlings and Brent geese, to name a few. As the sea today physically shapes the coast, so it has also shaped Felixstowe's history and identity.

I talked to one of the town's teenagers about her perception of the town. "There's not much for young people," she said. "I'll probably move away".
"And will you come back?" I asked.
"I don't know," she said. "But I'll always want to live near the sea".

Bibliography

Boyle, Audrey, Christine Luxton. (2001) **Watching Wildlife in Suffolk**. Suffolk Wildlife Trust.

Hegarty, Cain, Sarah Newsome (2007) **Suffolk's Defended Shore, Coastal Fortifications from the Air**. Swindon: English Heritage.

Hussey, Frank (1983) **Suffolk Invasion, the Dutch attack on Landguard Fort 1667**. Suffolk: Terence Dalton.

Malster, Robert (1992) **Felixstowe, a Pictorial History**. Chichester: Phillimore.

Messent Claude JW (1934). **The Monastic Remains of Norfolk and Suffolk**. Norwich:A.R.I.B.A.

Park, Cynthia. (2007) **The Cotman Walk, A Town Trail**. Felixstowe: the Felixstowe Society.

William Page, ed. (1907) **The Victoria History of the Counties of England Vol. 1**. Victoria County History.

Paul Pattison (2006) **Landguard Fort**. London: English Heritage.

Rayner, Doreen. (1991) **Walton Cum Felixstowe**. Suffolk: the author.

White.W. (1884) **Directory of Suffolk**.

Whitworth C, A.Muchal, R.Eccles, G.Fox. (1992) **Walking around Felixstowe**. Felixstowe: Felixstowe Society.

Wren, Wilfrid J (1976) **Ports of the Eastern Counties**. Lavenham: Dalton.

Wyllie, Neil, Peter White John Smith, and Phil Hadwen (2003). **Village Life in and Around Felixstowe**. John Wylie

Websites

www.portoffelixstowe.co.uk

www.visitfelixstowe.co.uk

www.wikipedia.org

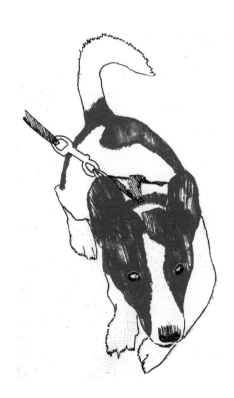